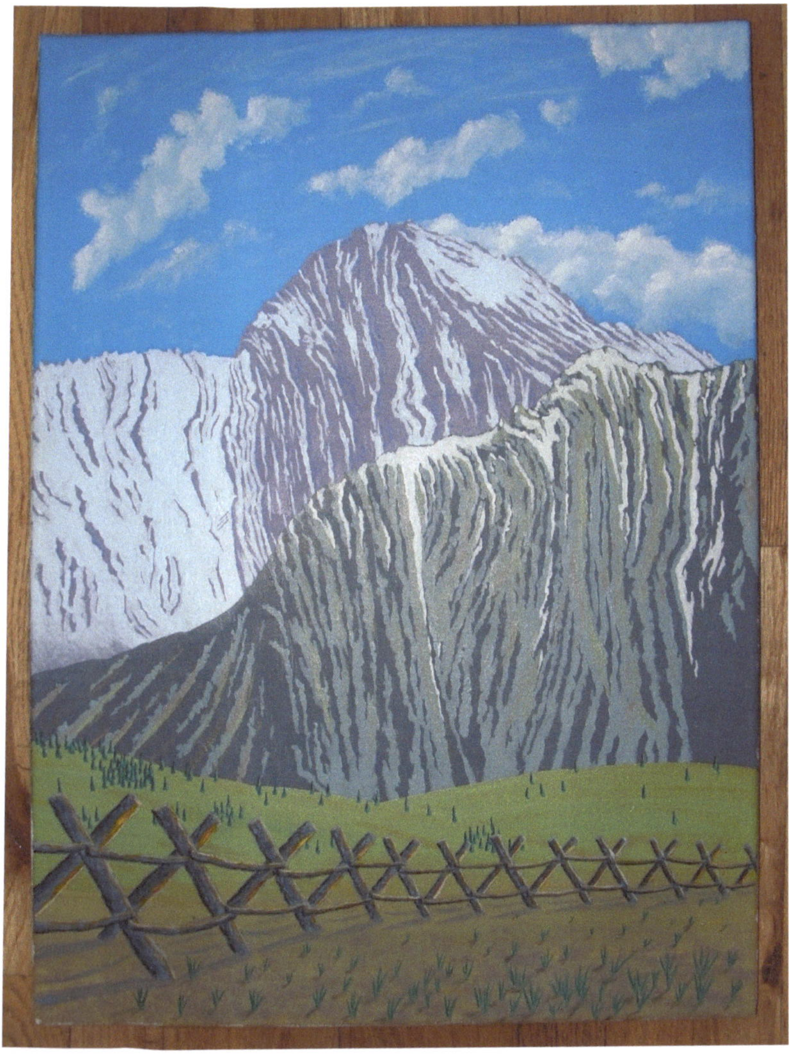

Mount Corruption

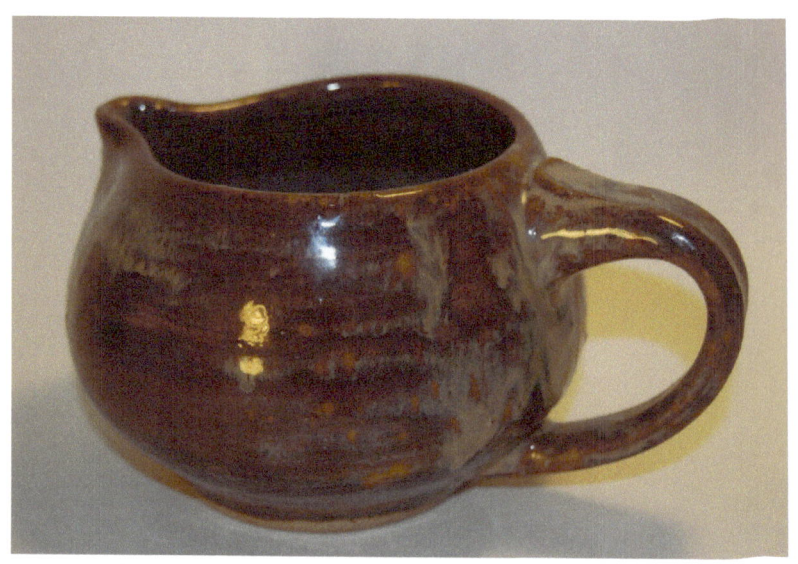

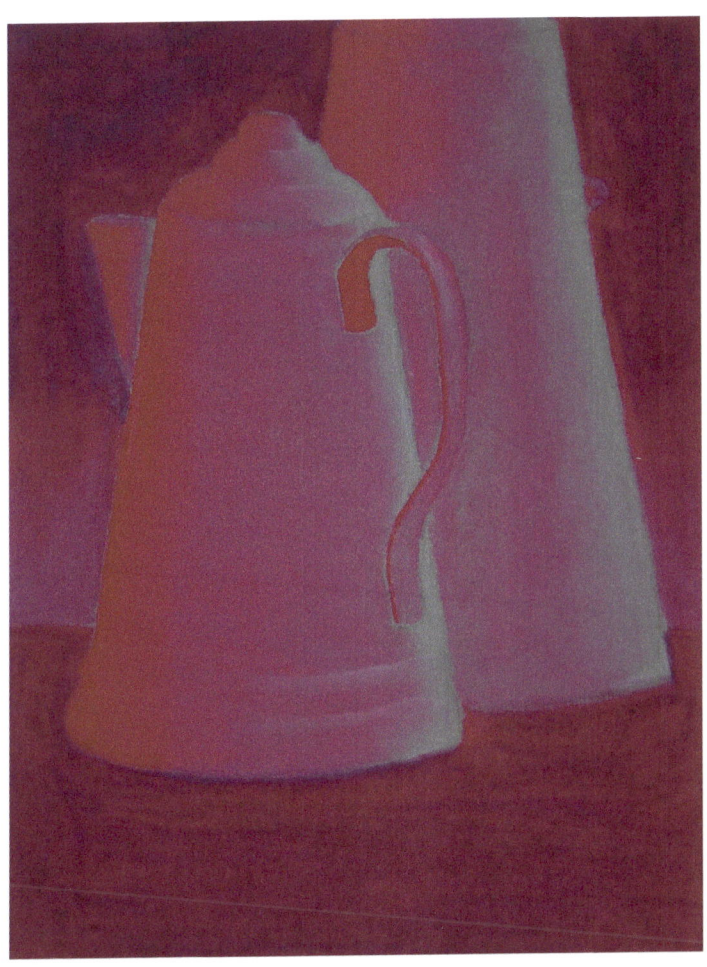

Still life with pitcher

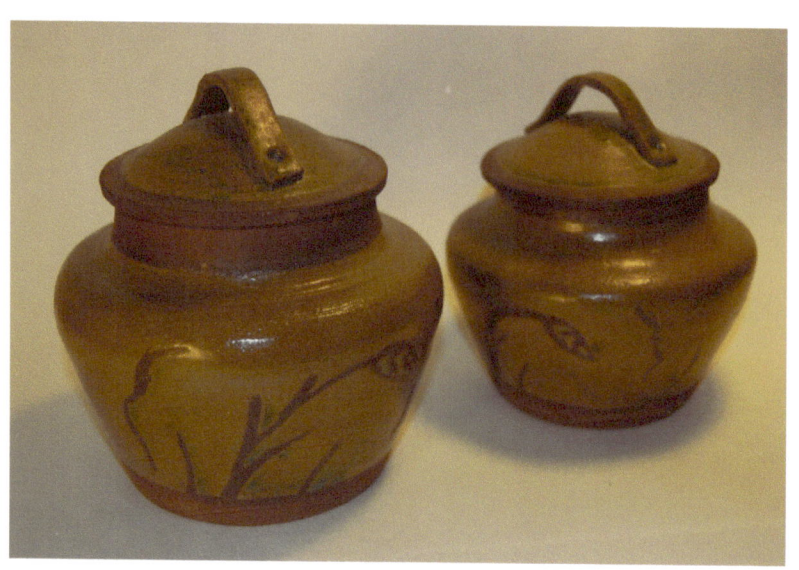

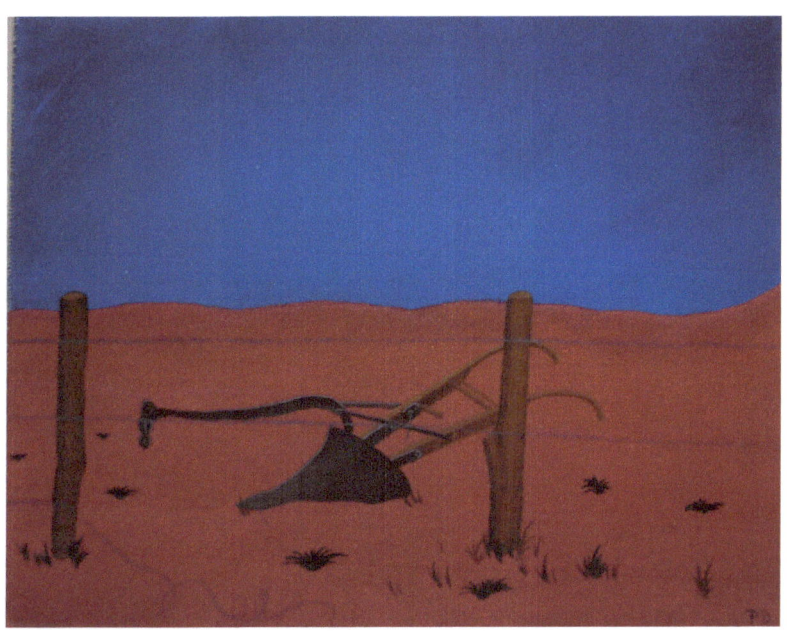

Abandoned Plow

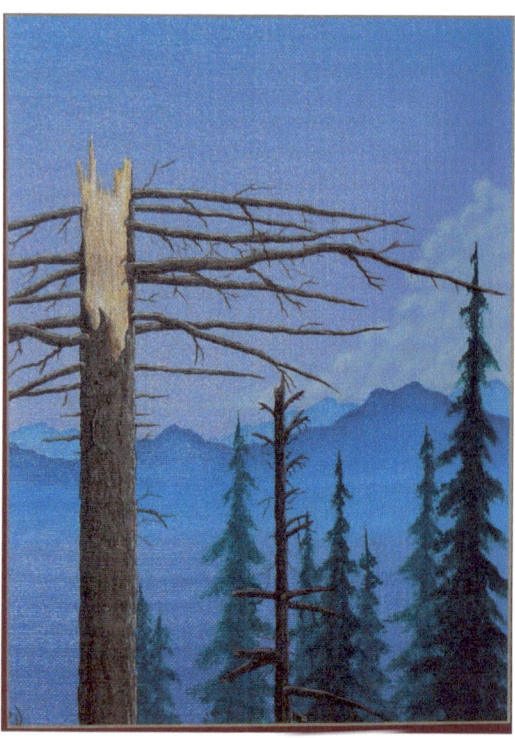

Broken Tree

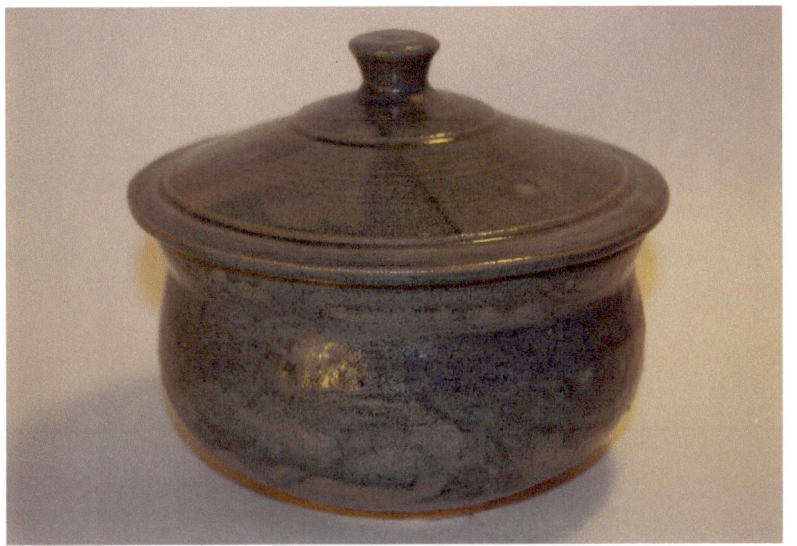

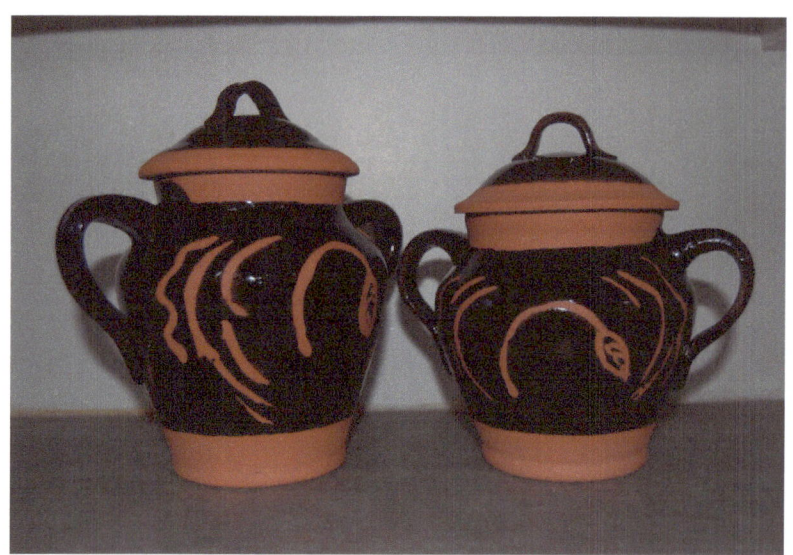

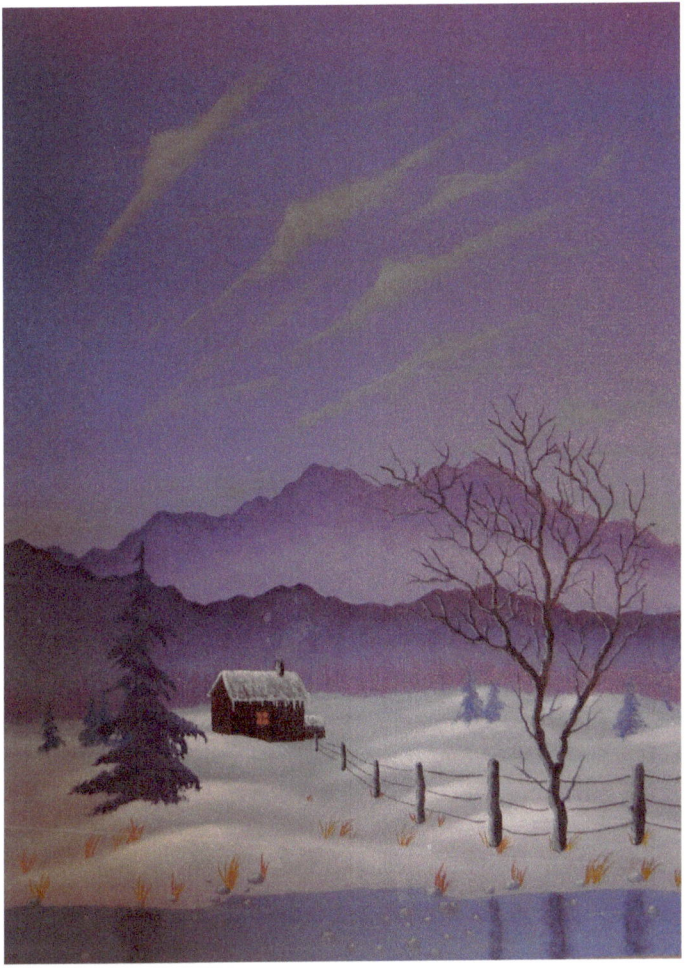

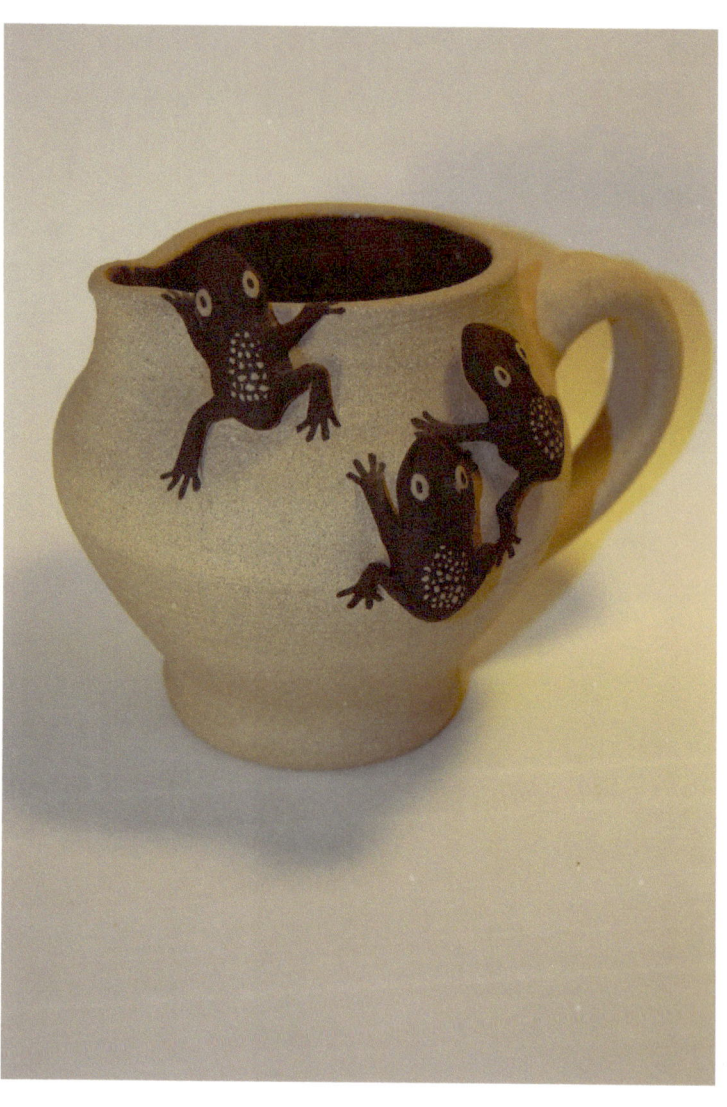

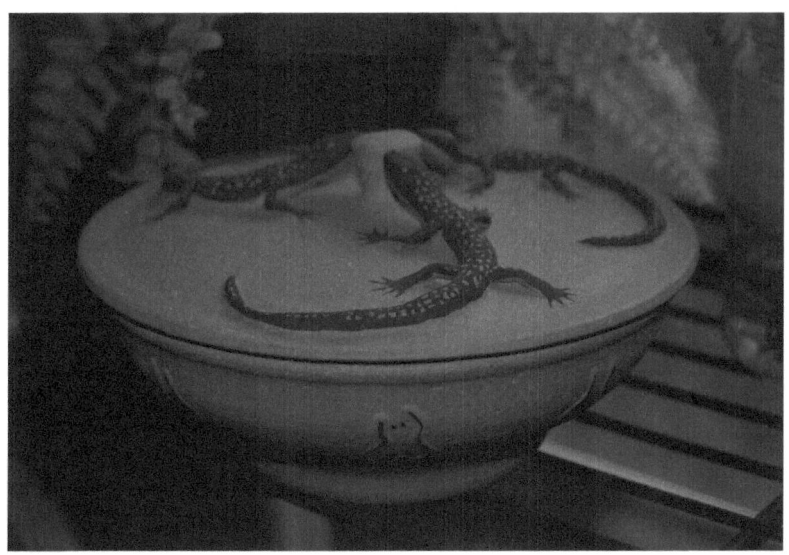

Lizard Bowl

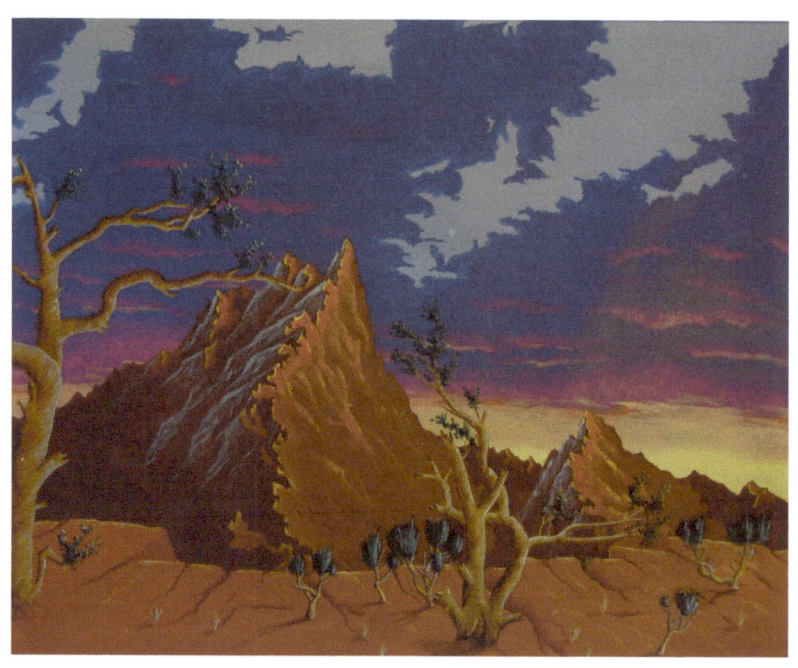

Sunset Landscape

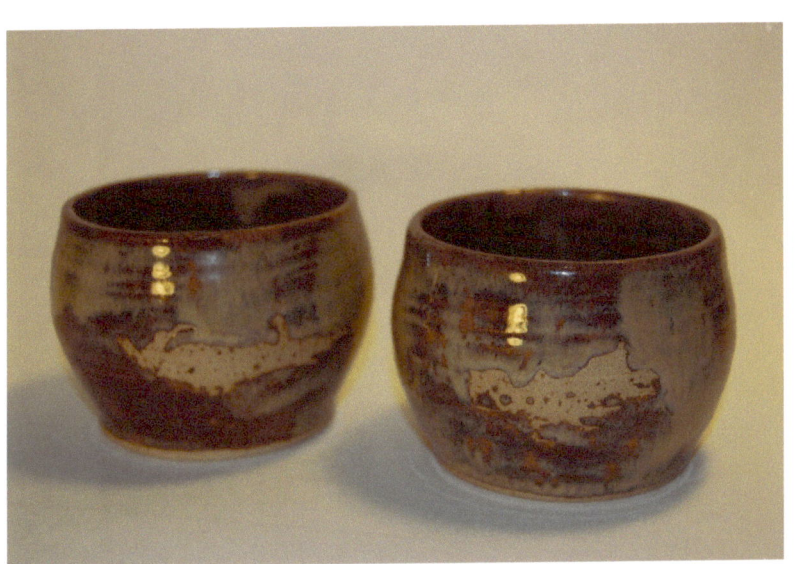

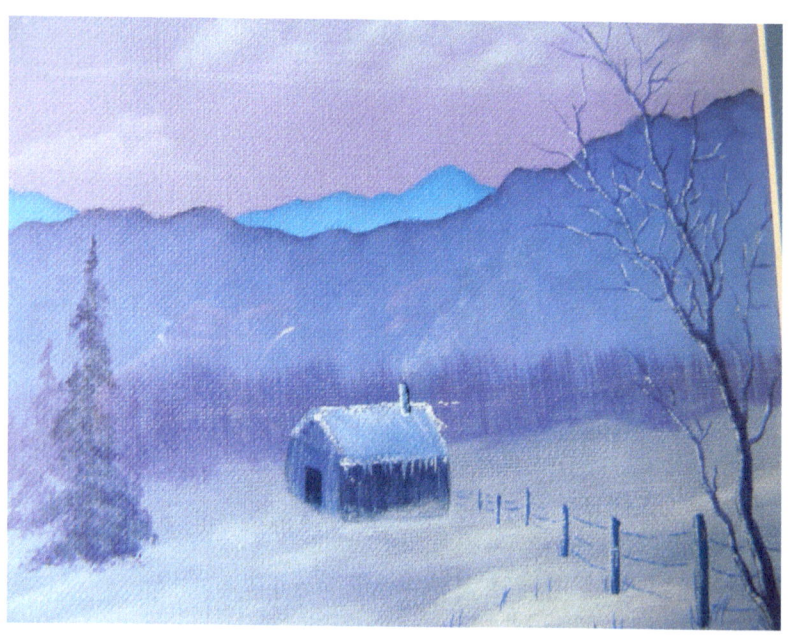

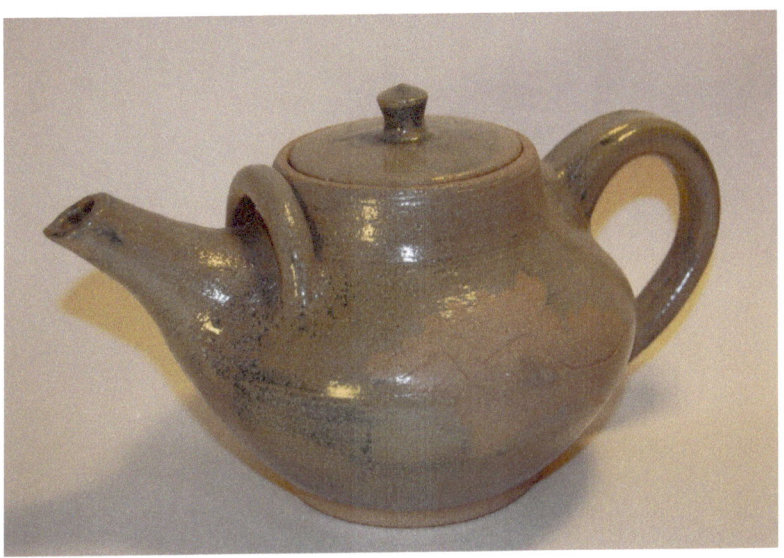

Teapot

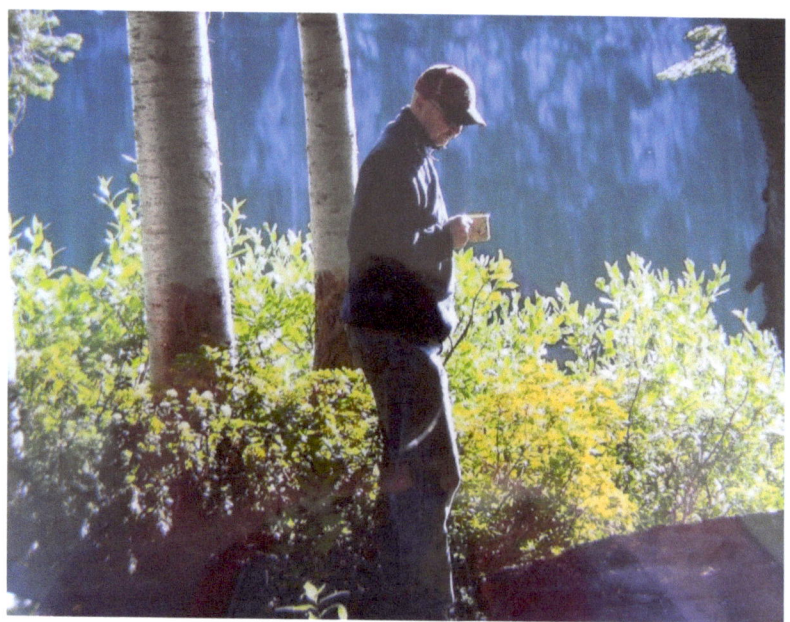

Jim Clark, mountains of Idaho

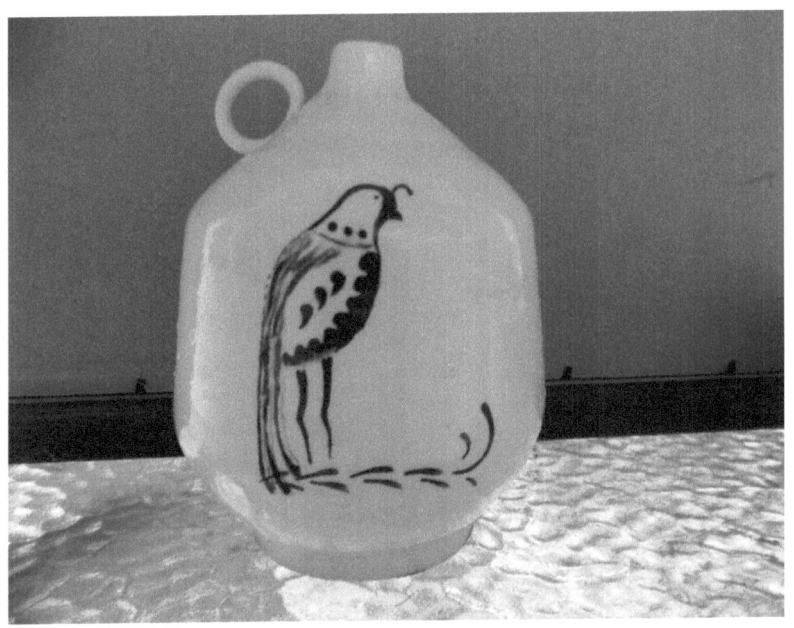

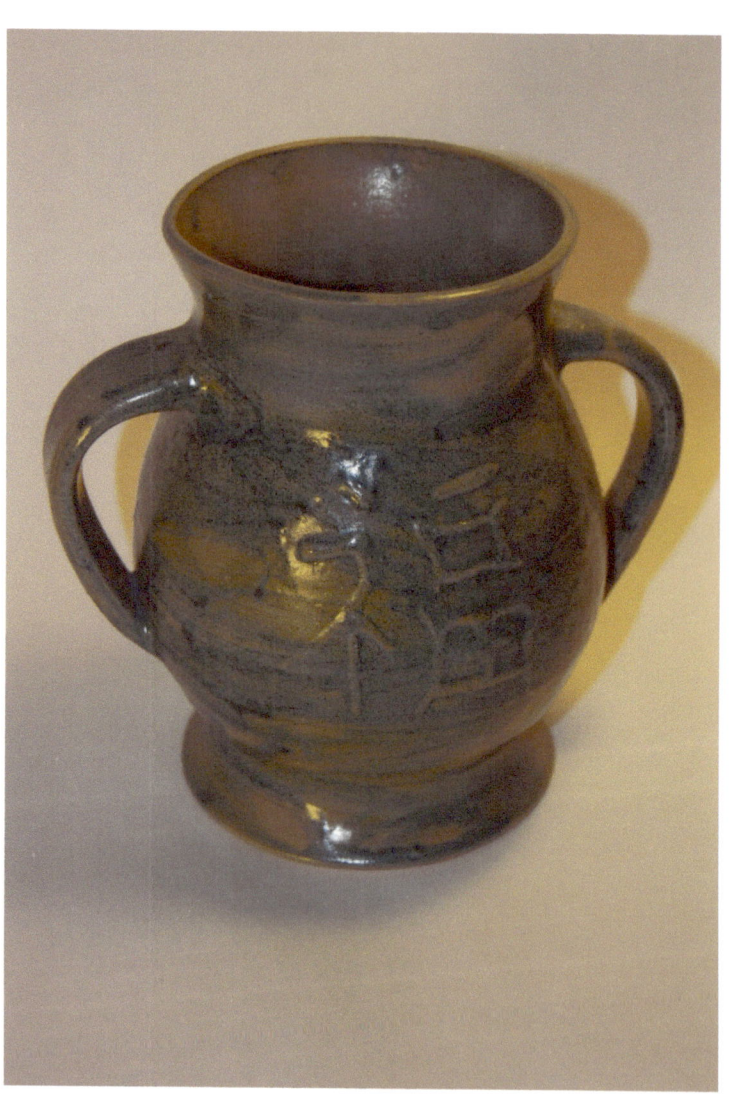

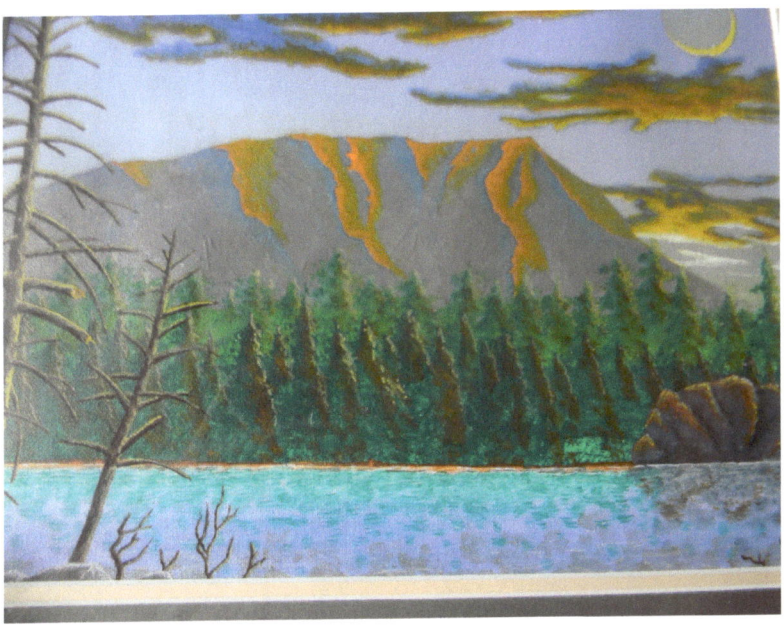

Langer Lake, Idaho

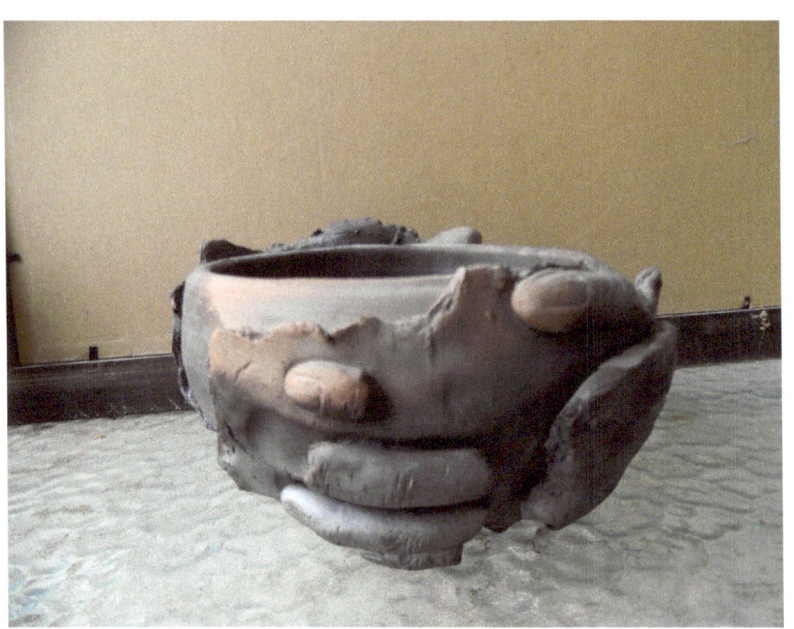

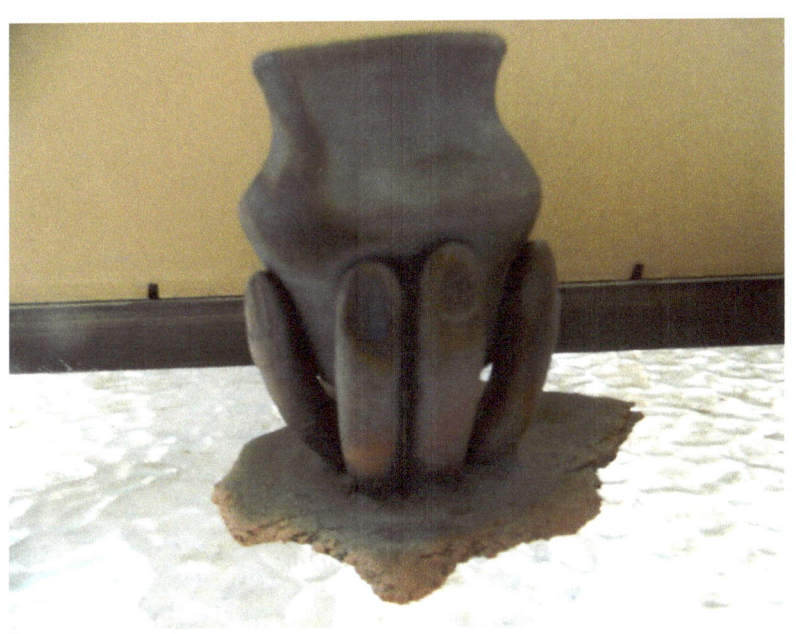

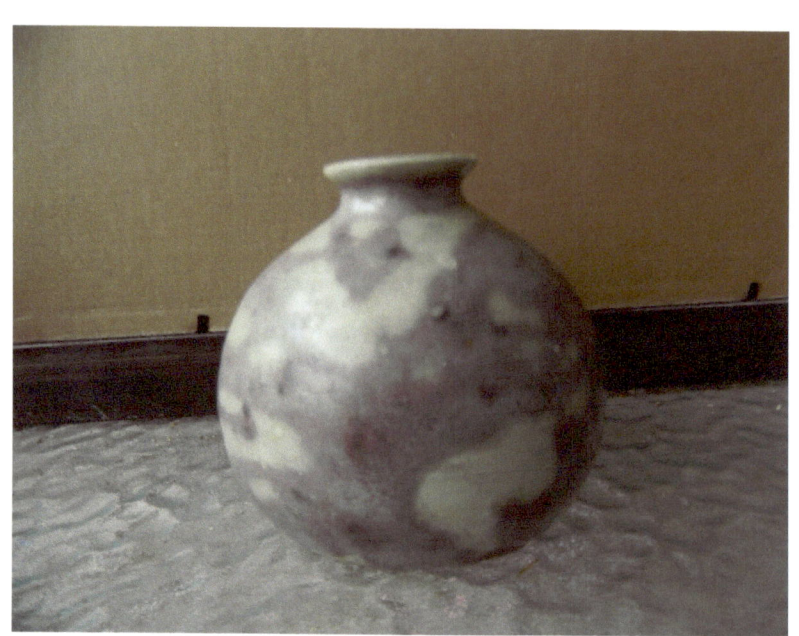

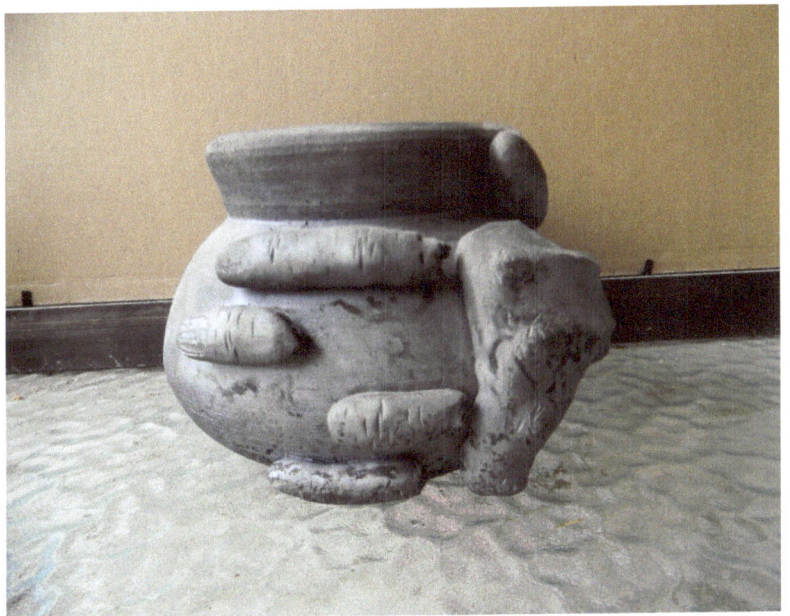

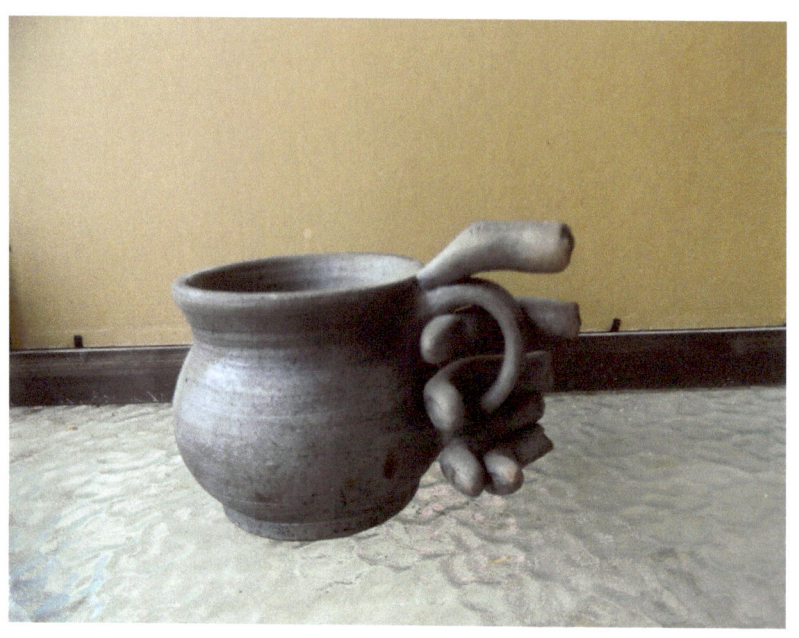

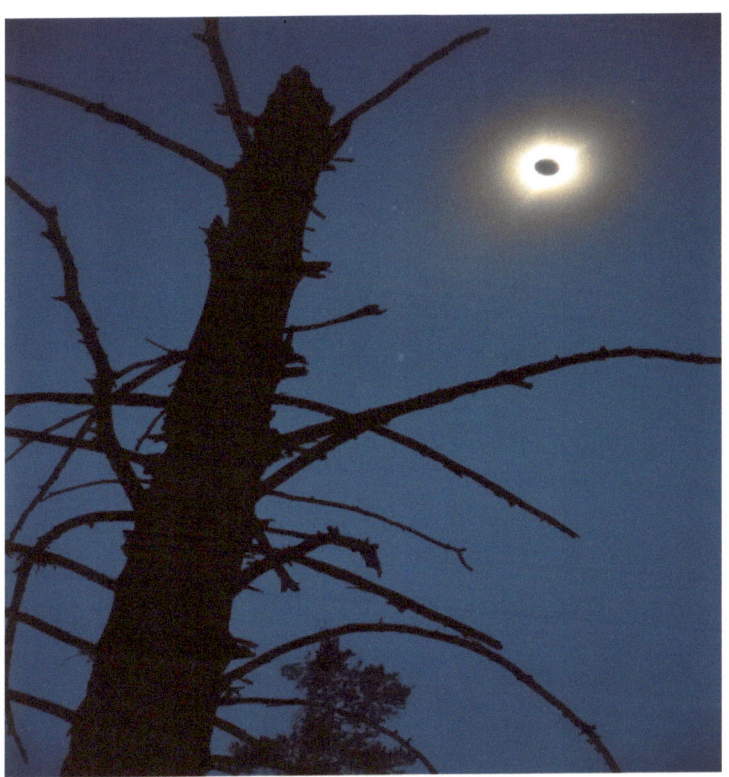

The Eclipse, 2017, Boise Idaho

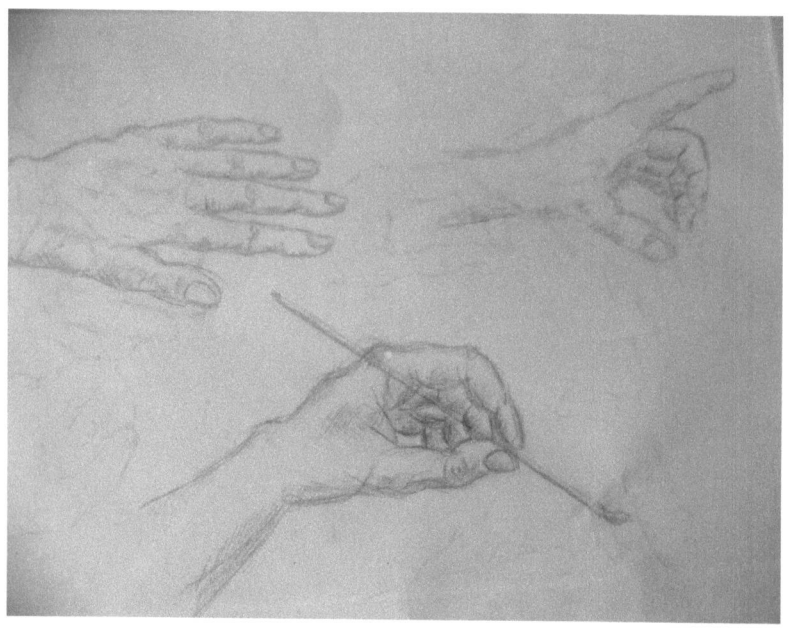

A study of hands

www.ingramcontent.com/pod-product-compliance
Lightning Source LLC
Chambersburg PA
CBHW040349220526
45473CB00009B/2819